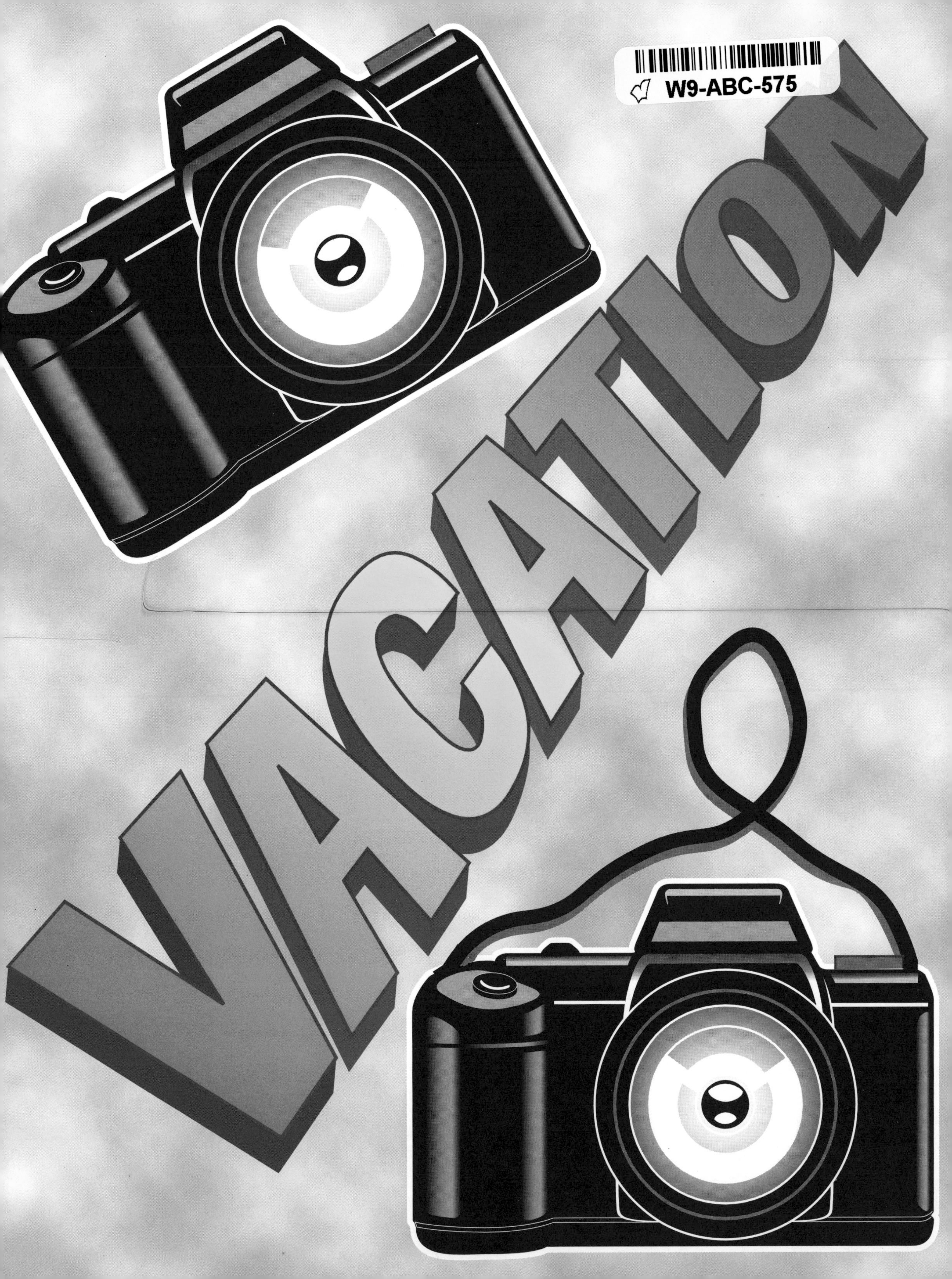
VACATION

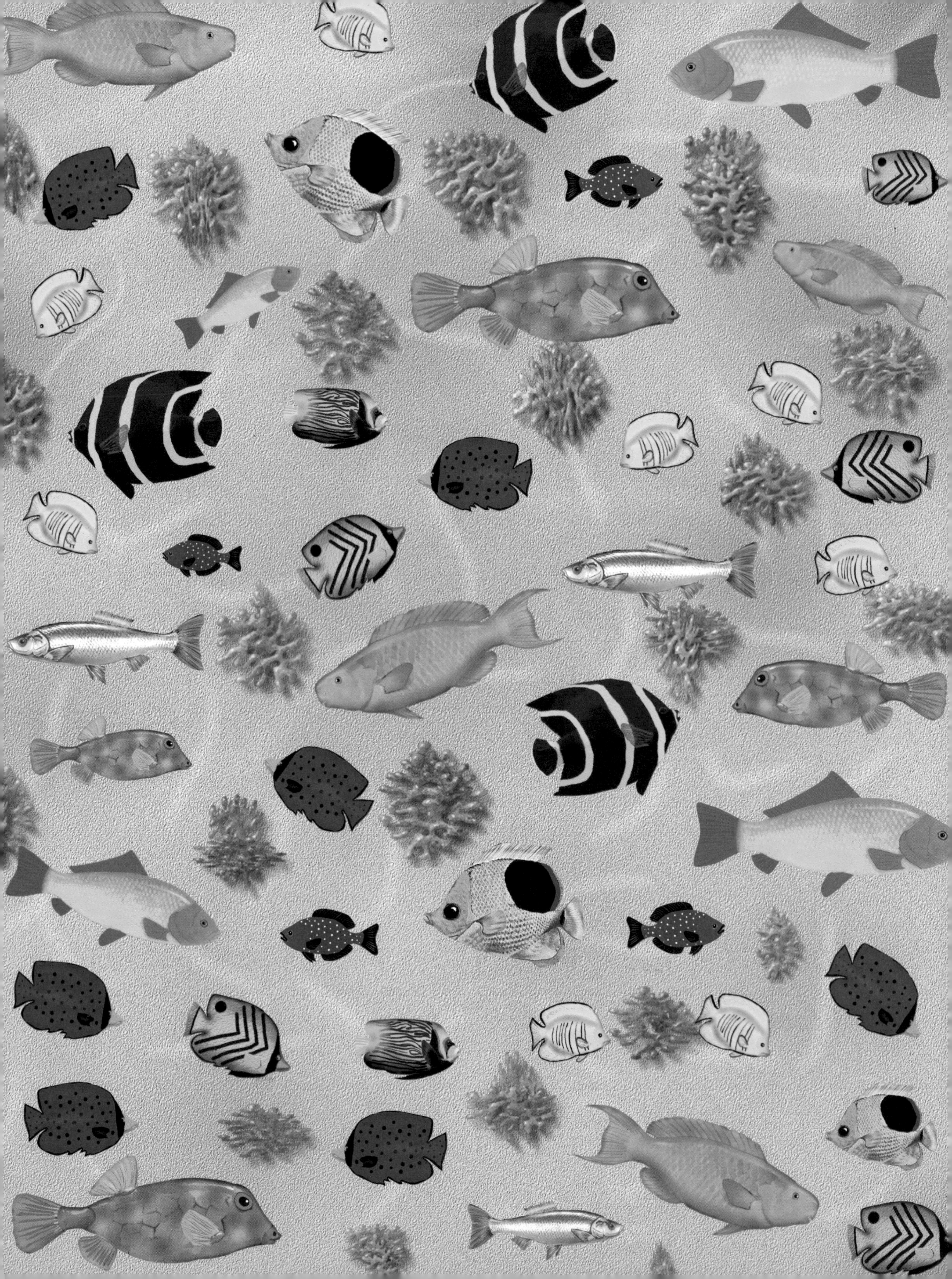

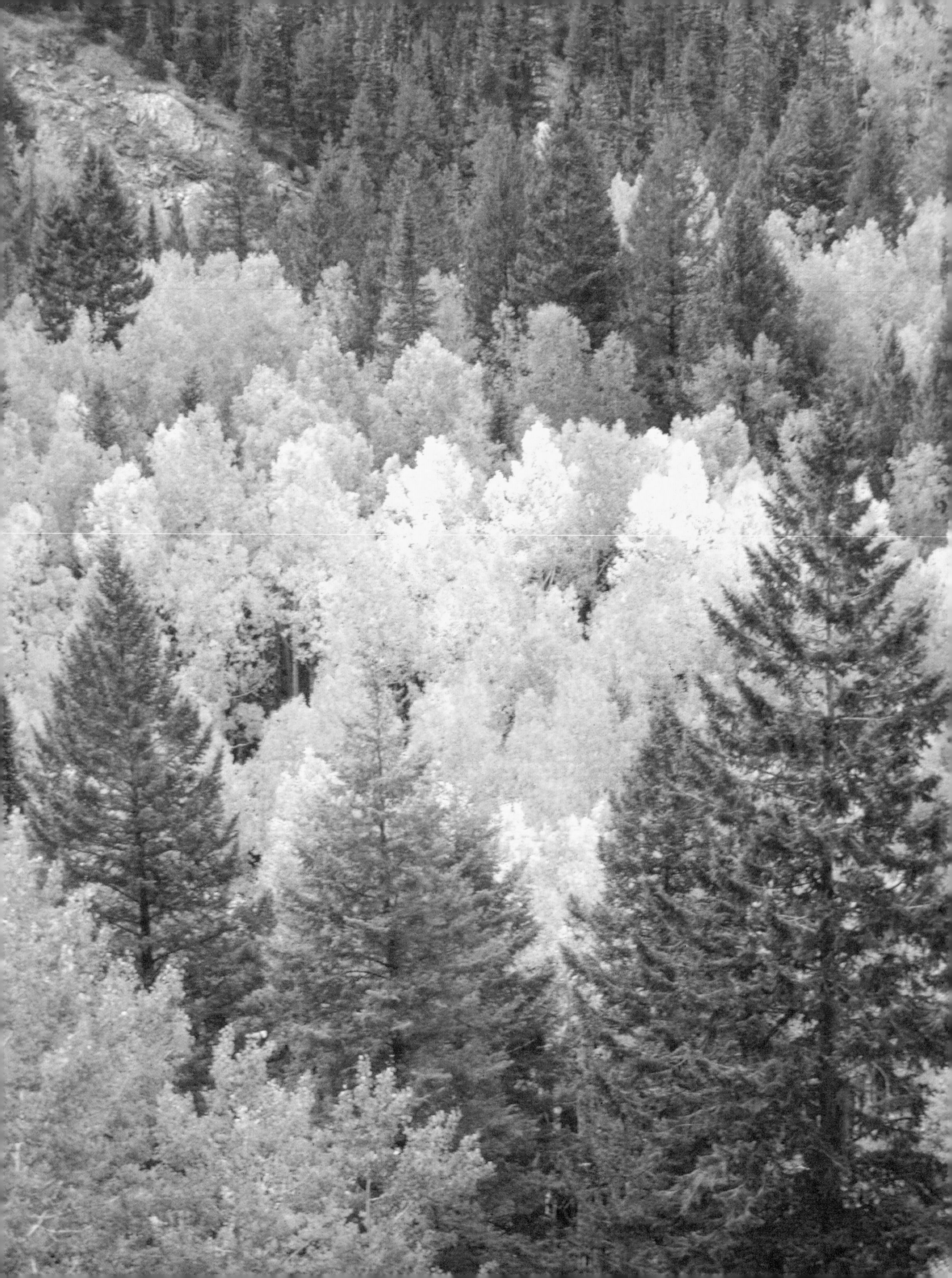

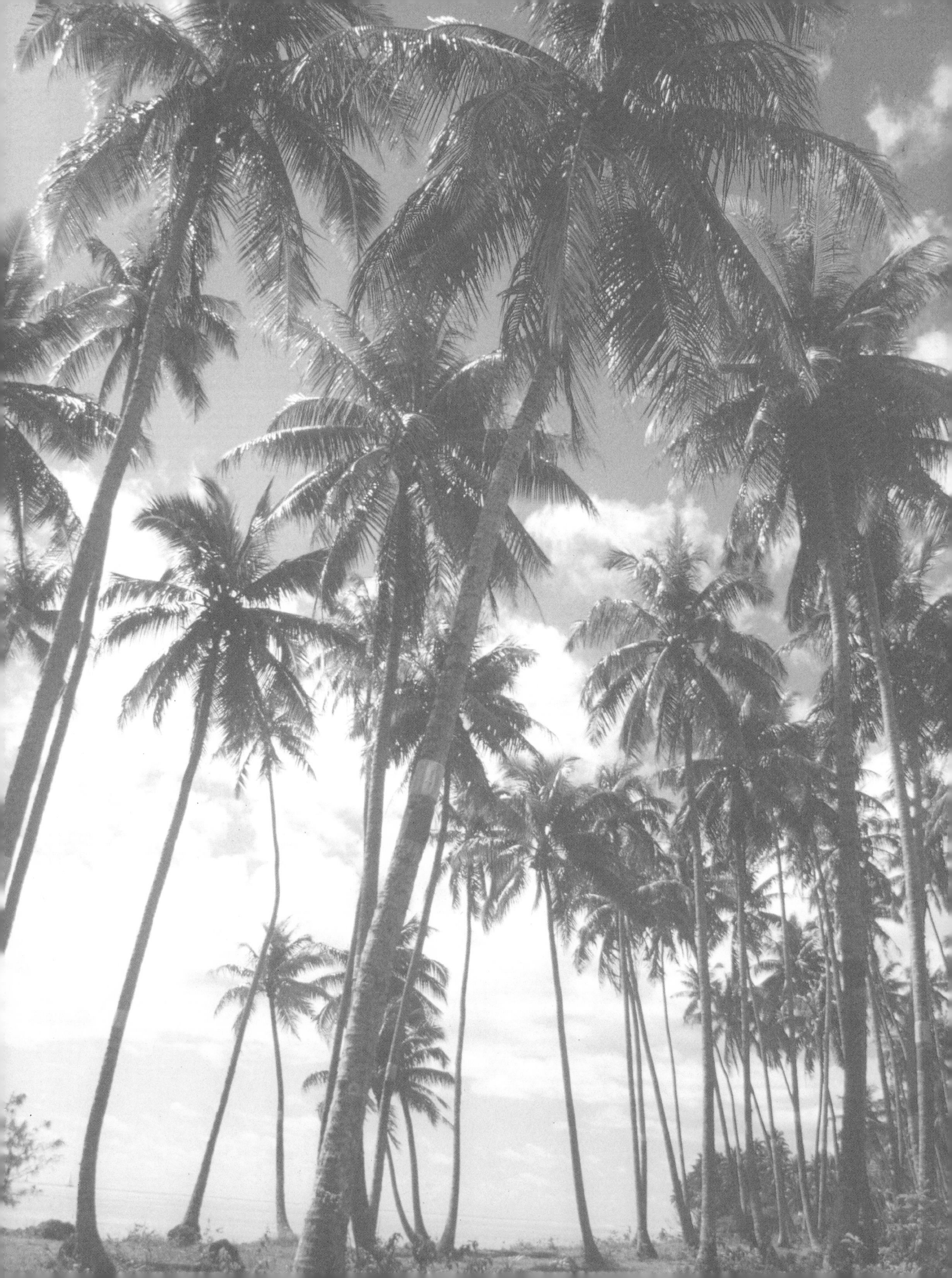

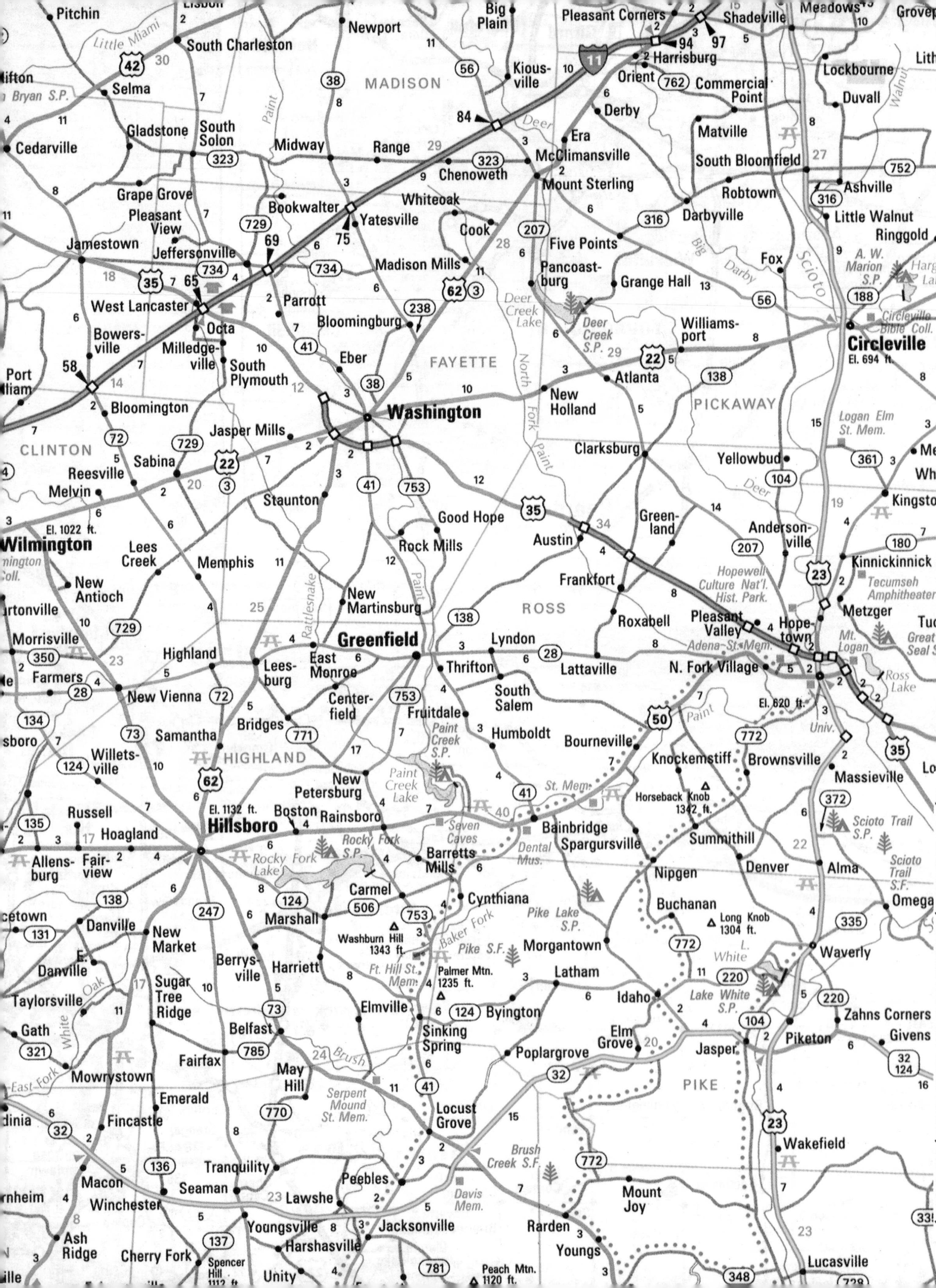

map from Rand McNally Road Atlas Deluxe 1997 edition ©1996 by Rand McNally

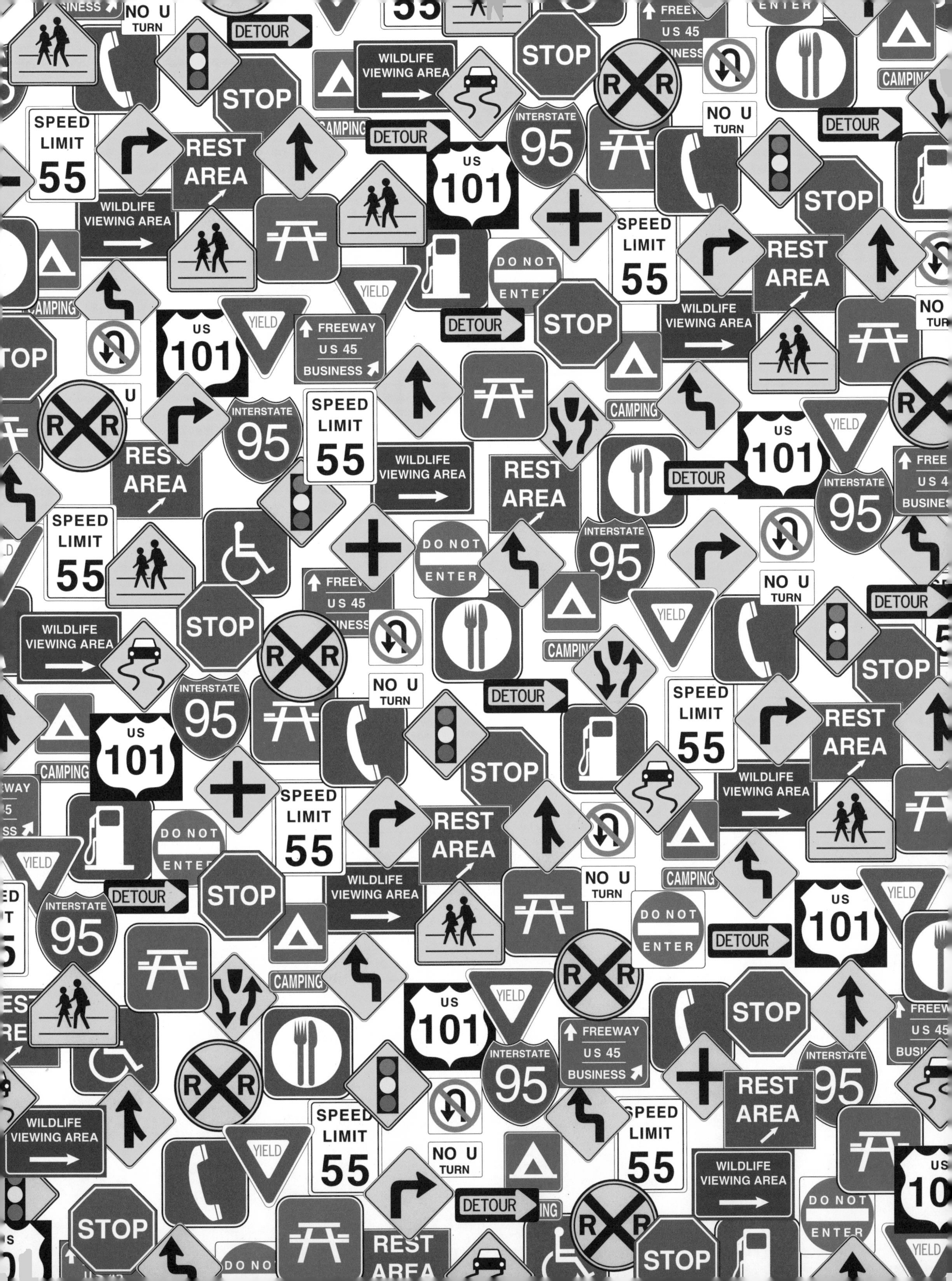

NO U TURN
DETOUR
WILDLIFE VIEWING AREA
STOP
SPEED LIMIT 55
REST AREA
CAMPING
INTERSTATE 95
US 101
YIELD
DO NOT ENTER
FREEWAY US 45 BUSINESS

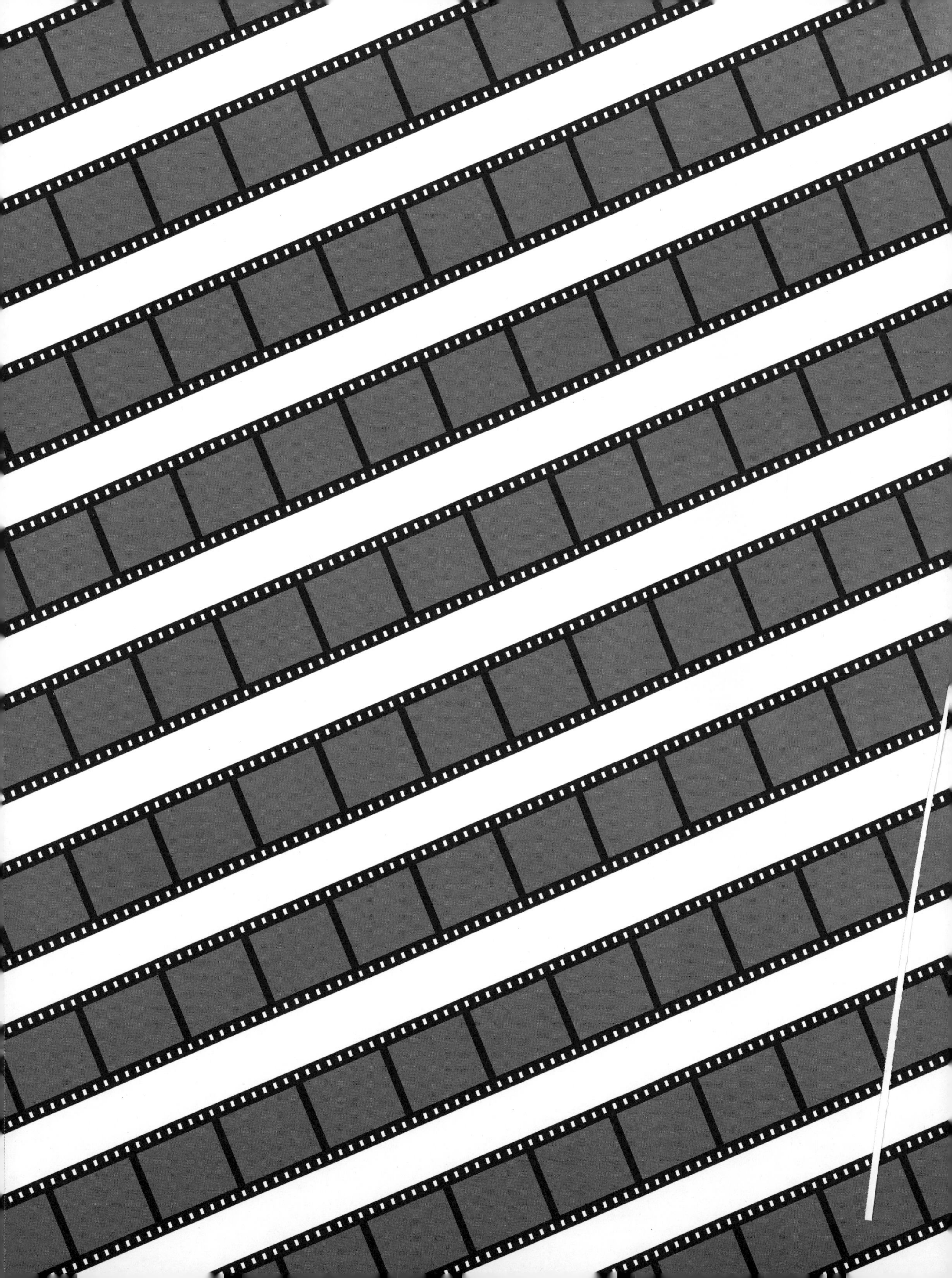

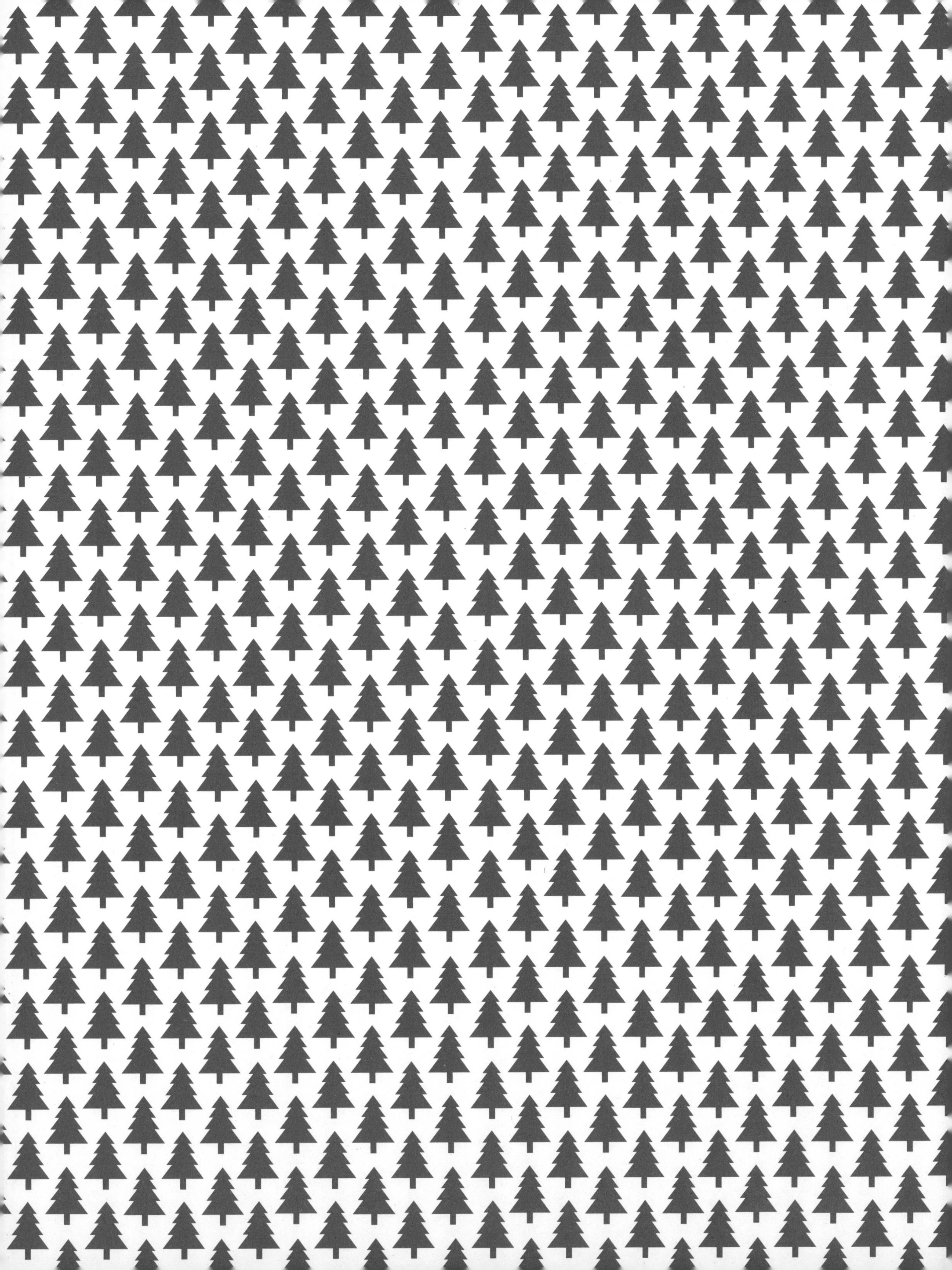